Solar Power

Energy for the Future

Written and illustrated by

Scott Andrew Robinson

Solar Power

Energy for the Future

written and illustrated by

Scott Andrew Robinson

Copyright 2015 Scott Andrew Robinson

All rights reserved

Library of Congress Control Number: 2015913671

ISBN-13: 978-1515232131

ISBN-10: 1515232131

CreateSpace Independent Publishing Platform,

North Charleston, SC

DEDICATION

This book is dedicated to my mother, because she gave me the idea for making a children's book about Solar Power. I would like the children to learn more about Solar Power, so that it would develop faster and be more cheaper and affordable so we will use it more in the future and save the environment and not spend any money.

I hope the world will have a greener solar powered future.

Solar Power: Energy for the Future

In the clear blue sky, there is one thing shining. That thing is the sun.

The sun is a star like the other stars you can see in the sky at night. It is closer to us than the other stars in the sky.

The sun is a burning ball of hot burning gases like the other stars. It is 1 million times bigger than the Earth. It is very hot at the surface and it is at its hottest in its center or core.

Inside the sun's core, a reaction takes place. The heat causes some atoms to move very fast. They fuse together into greater atoms and that releases energy. The energy moves into the surface of the sun. This causes the sun to shine.

Since the sun warms the Earth, all life can grow on Earth. So all energy comes from the sun.

Long ago, there were great forests and swamps on Earth. After the plants and animals no longer lived, what was left developed into coal, oil and gas.

Today, we use the gas to fuel our cars, trucks and buses. We use the coal and oil to heat our homes. Power plants burn coal to make electricity.

Over time, coal, oil and gas have been bad for the Earth. They give off gases that pollute the air and harm our world. These sources cannot be used forever. The sun is an energy source that will be available for millions of years.

The energy from the sun is one of the alternate renewable clean energy sources.

Some people use the sun's energy to heat homes. The glass lets the sun's energy go through and traps some of the heat and uses it to warm the house.   Black walls absorb more of the heat from the sun.

Some people use the sun's energy to heat water. There are flat solar panels on the roofs of houses. The sun heats the water in the panels. The heated water travels through the pipes and into the house for use.

Some power plants make electricity from the Sun's heat. Often these mirrors are focused to reflect the sun's light into tubes to heat the liquid. The heated liquid travels to where water is stored. It heats the water into steam which makes electricity.

There is another way to make electricity from the sun. The solar panels are made of silicon which is made from sand. When sunlight strikes this, electricity is made.

Someday cars will run on the energy of the sun. They might in the future have solar panels to do this.

There are some problems with solar energy. It can only be produced on clear sunny days and not on cloudy days and at night. Also, the silicon of the solar panels can produce little energy.

Batteries may store the sun's energy.

Scientists and companies are discovering new materials and ways to make solar cells that are cheaper and get more energy from the sun someday.

31

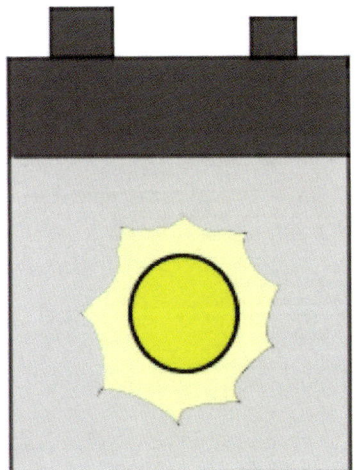

With those new discoveries and ideas, the world could move to solar power and stop using coal, oil and gas. Our earth will be greener and healthier. Solar Power could be one of the greatest sources of energy in the future.

Sources of Information:

The Sun our Nearest Star (Let's Read and Find Out About Science) © 1961, 1988, 2002
- Branley, Franklyn M. Miller, Edward
- HarperCollinsPublishers – New York City, New York
- Pages 6, 14, 20

A Refreshing Look at Renewable Energy with Max Axiom Super Scientist © 2010
- Krohn, Katherine Martin, Cynthia Schulz, Barbara
- Capstone Press – Mankato, Minnesota
- Pages 9-10

Renewable Energy (Energy Essentials) © 2004
- Saunders, Nigel Chapman, Steven
- Raintree – Chicago, Illinois
- Pages 14-15, 17

Renewable Energy Sources (Sci-Hi) © 2010
- Solway, Andrew
- Raintree – Chicago, Illinois
- Pages 22-25

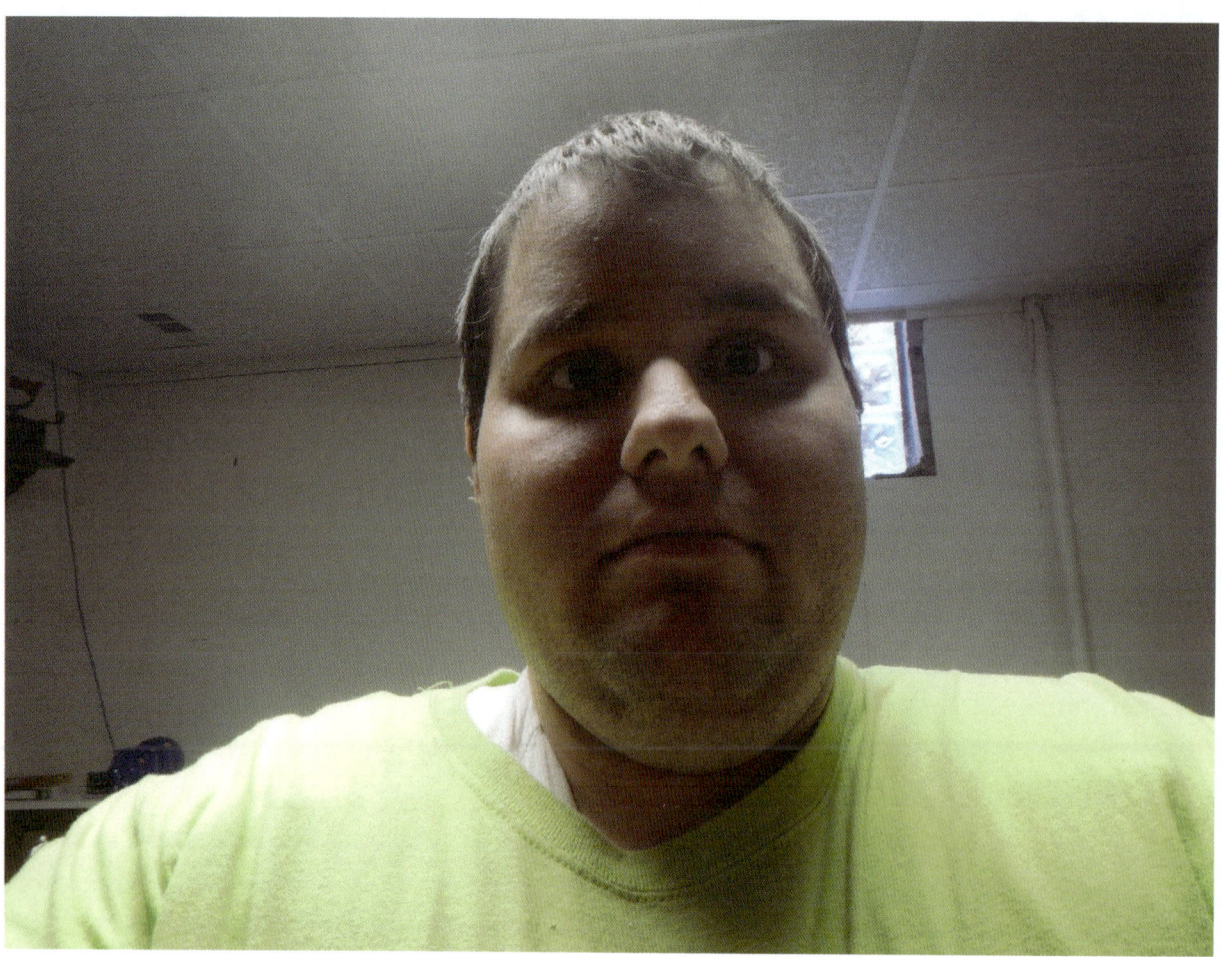

Dear Reader,

    I made this book about Solar Power. This will be the first children's book about Solar Power. If children learn more about Solar power. It will be cheaper and affordable in the future. I drew the illustrations for the book and even the cover using Manga Studio 5.0. I am autistic and I am working and learning at Goodwill now. I hope that if solar power could be cheaper and affordable, we will save more money and there will be more jobs.

    I would like solar power to be cheaper and affordable. Please read and enjoy this book.

Scott Andrew Robinson

Made in the USA
Lexington, KY
29 September 2015